DUCK

TIME

By: JENNIFER KENDIS
ANDERSON

This book is dedicated to my niece Eva Gijon. Thank you for giving me inspiration and ideas when I get writer's block and need help getting my idea light bulb to turn on. I love you very much.

"Grandma, Grandma, can we feed the ducks?"

"Not yet they are in the nest. We have to wait for the momma duck to lead them to the water, and then we can."

"Why not now, the nest is over in the rose bushes? It is very close Grandma please?"

"NO you never go near a nest. If you do the momma duck will get scared and leave the babies because she thinks you did something to them to hurt them."

"We would never do that Grandma."

"We know that but the ducks don't."

"Grandma I don't understand they come right up to us and almost take the food right out of our hand's when they are in the canal and we are on the boat dock, they know us."

"Yes in the water they come up to us because they feel safe but in the nest it is like well how would you feel if you were sleeping and someone broke into the house?"

"Very scared, now I understand Grandma."

"So we will wait until they go in the water."

"Well when will that be Grandma?"

"When they are ready, just look out the window and when you see them in the canal let me know."

"Grandma while we are waiting would you tell me about ducks or at least our ducks, please?"

"Our ducks?"

"Yes I know they are wild ducks and they live at your house in your rose bushes but I only get to see them when we come to visit you but I like to call them ours because they could have chosen anyone's roses but they chose ours so they are ours."

"Well that's a fair answer. I can tell you about them but you can learn more than I know by looking them up in the encyclopedia."

"The encyclowhat?"

"The book we used before the internet, or just use the internet or the discovery channel probably has a duck documentary."

"Yes Grandma but if you tell me it is like you are telling me a story and a real story and not just one of those "And they lived happily ever after" stories, Grandma I am so over the Princess thing."

"Ha Ha you are so silly."

"Please Grandma?"

"Ok there are many different kinds of ducks. The ones we have are called

"Mallards". An adult male and female duck meet, they fall in love."

"Ducky love how cute?"

"Then they find a safe place to build a nest. They need a place close to water but away from danger like roads and too many people. They choose places like the rose bushes because they are small enough to go under the thorns but foxes and cats can't get them."

"Foxes and cats oh no poor ducky's."

"Yes that is why the rose bushes or some kind of a safe place like that. The female duck lays a bunch of eggs. She sits on them to keep them warm until they hatch."

"Hatch Grandma?"

"When the egg shells break open so the baby ducks can come out."

"Oh I got it."

"When she gets hungry the daddy duck will switch places with her so the mommy duck can eat. When the eggs hatch the mommy duck stays with them always until the babies are big enough to leave the nest so the parents can teach them how to find food, safety, and how to swim. While she is there the daddy will bring them all food since they can't go get it yet. When they are bigger they all go together to look for food. They walk and swim in a line so they don't get lost. In the line either the mommy or the daddy walks in front and the other walks at the back of the line to keep everyone straight."

"Grandma how come the babies have a yellow fluffy colored stuff instead of big feathers that are pretty brown or green like the big ducks?"

"All ducks have the soft fuzziness on them it is called "Down"; the feathers grow in over it. The babies are born without feathers they grow in later. It's kind of like when your two sisters were born they had only a little hair now they both have long brown pretty hair with some curls."

"By the way where are your two sisters?"

"Downstairs watching cartoons with mom."

"No Grandma I love cartoons I just wanted to see the ducks and hear you tell me about them. They are the only pets we have."

"Wait."

"I know Grandma they are wild and are not pets but it is the closest thing we have."

"Ok well as long as you understand they are wild and not pets."

"Yes I do, is it time yet?"

"No not yet."

"Grandma is it time yet?"

"Yes now it is, go get your mom and sisters and I will get the food, then we can go feed the ducks."

"I am ready Grandma."

"Where is everyone else?"

"They are watching a movie."

"Don't you want to watch it too?"

"No way Grandma, it is a baby's movie, anyway I saw it already like a 100 times, and I love feeding the ducks, so I am ready, Grandma."

"Ok me too let's go. I will hold the food but can you hold my hand?"

"I'm a big girl grandma but I like holding your hand so you don't get lost in the backyard."

"You are so silly but as long as you hold my hand, ok."

"Grandma Look they are swimming over to us. They must be hungry?"

"Yes they are all coming over."

"I hope they like the food? It is in a can."

"That is because I went to the pet store and got special food for feeding wild birds like those ducks. It has lots of vitamins and good things the ducks need to grow big, strong, and healthy."

"Oh No Grandma you mean you bought duck vegetables, that's not good they won't want to eat from us anymore Grandma."

"Trust me it will be fine."

"Grandma some of the ducks are swimming over to the other side of the canal, someone is feeding them too. They are feeding them bread. Once they tell the other ducks bread or vegetables they will leave us."

"Trust me I promise it will be fine."

"Look Grandma they love it and the others are coming back. That is funny Grandma the ducks like vegetables more than bread."

"I told you to trust me."

"I know I am sorry Grandma."

"It's ok, look at the babies; they have started getting the adult feathers."

"Yes Grandma I think they will be real pretty soon, right now they look silly with half feathers and half fluffy stuff."

"Once they grow all in and get bigger they will fly south for the winter to warmer weather. The northern ducks will fly south too. This to them is warmer weather."

"Grandma we don't get to visit you that often will I get to see the winter ducks? And can we feed them too?"

"I hope you get to see them and yes we can feed them too. That is enough food for today. I am sorry you have to leave in the morning. I wish you could stay longer than the weekend but you girls have school and your Grandfather and I have to work."

"Grandma I think this is so cool."

"What?"

"We came to visit when the ducks were building the nest in the rose bushes. Then we came to visit when they had the eggs. I remember because we got to watch from the window in the dining room. Then we came to visit when they were big enough to go out and swim. Now we are visiting when they are starting to get their big duck feathers. I can't wait to visit during the next part."

"The way you said that it's like you only come to see the ducks?"

"No Grandma we came to see you guys. The ducks are just an extra bonus part."

"It's ok I was only teasing you."

"GRANDMA you are the one who is silly."

"Let's go inside now. You will be leaving in the morning and hopefully coming back in a few months, if not sooner."

"Grandma I just told everyone what they missed."

"Were they disappointed?"

"No they didn't even realize we were gone and back."

"Grandma I want to give you a big hug now since we are leaving in the morning."

"OK."

"Grandma, Grandma, we are back finally. I didn't think we would ever get here, it was snowing the whole time."

"Well I am glad you are here."

"Me too Grandma, me too, Grandma how are the ducks? With school Mom said this was the soonest we could come back."

"They already got their big duck feathers and flew south for the winter. The other ducks are here now. They are almost all white not like our other ducks that were green and brown. They flew down from the north so this is their warm weather."

"This? Crazy ducks it's snowing."

"Yes but it snows a lot more and gets a lot colder where they are from."

"Grandma it is still snowing. Are we going to be able to feed the ducks in the snow?"

"No we are not going outside while it is snowing just to feed the ducks we will wait until it stops."

"Grandma everyone is watching television. Can I sit here with you up here in the sitting room and can we watch the ducks together?"

"Yes we can. That would make me very happy. Look out this window. See the canal is frozen over and the ducks are sitting on top of the ice."

Grandma it sure is a good thing they have feathers or my oh my their little ducky bottoms would be cold!"

"Yes that is true. Look the snow is melting as it hits the ice so it is turning into water. The ducks are just sitting there trying to keep warm; I guess it is warmer in the water than on the ice because if it was colder the water would have turned to ice too."

"Oh No Grandma that one duck is coming in for a landing. I don't think it sees the ice under the little bit of water."

"STRIKE!"

"Ha Ha it is like duck bowling. At first I was scared but now that I see that they are alright and only just slide around on the ice, well now it's just too funny. I almost want some more ducks to come and land so we can watch them slide all over the canal."

"Actually me too, that was pretty funny."

"Grandma our duck time is great. I think the only thing that would make it better besides being able to feed them today if it wasn't snowing was if instead of ducks they were pink flamingos. That would be real cool."

"Yes it would, I agree pink flamingos would be cool but they live much, much further south and I love our duck time too."

"I love you Grandma!"

"I love you too, Eva!"

www.ingramcontent.com/pod-product-compliance
Lightning Source LLC
Chambersburg PA
CBHW070527290526
45790CB00003B/1330